MAURICE HARMON

The Mischievous Boy

and other poems

salmonpoetry

Published in 2008 by

Salmon Poetry,

Cliffs of Moher, County Clare, Ireland

Website: www.salmonpoetry.com

Email: info@salmonpoetry.com

ISBN 978-1-903392-86-7

Cover design & typesetting: Siobhán Hutson
Cover illustration: Stained glass window titled
                                                 The Mischievous Boy by Phyllis Burke

for Séamus and Gabriel MacGabhann

Acknowledgements

I wish to thank the editors of the *Irish Times*, *Poetry Ireland Review* and the *Sewanee Review*, where some of these poems first appeared.

'The Glimmer Man' first appeared in Maurice Harmon, *Thomas Kinsella Designing for the Exact Needs*, 2008.

'The Gentle Years' appeared in *Salmon A Journey in Poetry 1981-2007*, edited by Jessie Lendennie, 2007.

'Dear Editor' appeared in *Maurice Harmon Selected Essays*, edited by Barbara Brown, 2006.

'Slipstream' was published in *Something Beginning with P.*, edited by Seamus Cashman, 2005.

'The Mischievous Boy' was written for the composer Derek Ball as a companion piece to his musical version of 'Prelude', *The Doll with Two Backs*, 2004.

'Shiki' is based on *Now, to Be! Shiki's Haiku. Moments for Us Today*, edited by Masako Hirai, 2003.

'Girl in a Pale Slip' was published in Maurice Harmon, *Tales of Death and Other Poems*, 2001.

'Lost for Words' and 'A Politician's Defence' are based on reports in the *Irish Times*. Sections vi and vii of 'Lost for Words' were published in Maurice Harmon, *The Book of Precedence*, a chapbook of political poems, 1994.

Many thanks to the Heinrich Böll Committee, who allowed me to enjoy the seclusion of the Heinrich Böll cottage in Achill, where some of these poems were written.

Contents

IV

V

I

A wind-swept spirit

A wind-swept spirit lives within this mortal frame
with nine holes and a hundred bones
torn by the slightest puff of air.

Years ago something in me took
to writing poetry, at first just to see
if I could do it, then it turned serious.

At times the spirit sank, almost ready
to quit. At times so puffed with pride
I was high as a kite, but that did not last.

To tell the truth ever since it started
I've never known peace, caught between
one doubt and another, one word and the next.

But knowing no other art the spirit
hangs on blindly doing the best it can
taking one step at a time.

The Glimmer Man

for TK

He has known this half-light
half a century
its blank space
its emptiness

Sitting together in his kitchen
his face soft as when in 86
we argued Thomas or MacNeice

He uses fewer words now
as I lean close I hear him mention
'the harried self'

As we touch stems
a pale light
hisses around us
like gas

In Two Minds

The question we used to ask was
How could you know so much about us?
The atmosphere and pressures of boarding school
The trust, the isolation
Dismal days that soaked the sensibility
Soutanic terror, a creepy crawly morality
Days when the whole school
Cringed in fear of sanctions and the strap

We did not see behind mimetic speech
Nor hear ironic footwork on the harmonium
Nor grasp depth-charges of the moral imagination

The self-conscious walk on the north side
Limned a mental world beyond the virgin's vigil
The mad nun and red-eyed Mulrennan
The unease when lice crawled along the collarbone.

You threw your cap at relics of ould decency
Assumed an identity and carried it off
In the orchestration of colours, clouds and moving creatures
The Italianate photo-op on the beach
The gasping vision of what you would come to be

Juggling two parts of his mind the man from Clogher
Also admitted disorder and misrule
Learned what he could from teachers and talkers
He knew red-rimmed eyes and enchantments
The Captain and the mad Mulrannys

He, too, turned to words, although with less assurance.
Your Grecian mask more subtle than his high-flown classicism.

Within such fabrications plainer truths
Feeling for language, an ear for ordinary speech.

You also returned to the literal
And lived in two places at the one time.

Dear Editor

I've been writing poetry since I was 12.
I'm a founder member of the Balscaddan Writers Association
and have received numerous prizes for my poetry.

I won the Stamullen Best Writer of the Year award
and was runner-up in the Gormanstown Annual Festival of
New Writing.

I have been given honourable mention in the Painestown
Creative Arts Competition. My poems have been published
in the *Little Gazette*, the *Mullingar Starling*, *The Glass Case*,
the *Statue*, the *Mind-Sweeper* and many other prestigious
journals, at home and abroad.

Three of my poems have been published on the Internet.
Seamus MacDall, a judge in the Gormanstown Festival, said
my poems 'have the ring of true sincerity'.

I would be thrilled to have my poems in your prestigious
periodical and chosen by you of all people.

I enclose just 16 but I have loads more if you'd like to read them.
I am preparing my first collection which will have about
140 poems.
Do you think is that enough?
I enclose a SAE in case you want to send some back.
I'm going to send them to another prestigious magazine.
Thanking you for your attention.

My mother says she went to the Arcadia with your father.
Isn't that a kick?
My husband says he marked you when you played top of
the left for Louth.

He says you were 'a dirty hoor'.

With best wishes,

Yours sincerely,
Jasmine.

P.S. That's the name of a flower.

Girl in a Pale Slip

Have you seen a girl

in a pale, shapeless,   washed-out blue slip,
under a short, bulky,   coarse fabric, off-white jacket,
over a pair of baggy,   crumpled, outsized,
dirty pants, over scuffed,   striped, thick-soled trainers?

I've walked out to find her
when the mist filters from the shore.

                         I've gone at nightfall
          where the blackthorn circles the mound.

I've rehearsed questions for her,
names of queens.

Have you seen a girl

in a pale, shapeless,   washed-out, blue slip,
under a short, bulky,   coarse fabric, off-white jacket,
over a pair of baggy,   crumpled, outsized,
dirty pants, over scuffed,   striped, thick-soled trainers?

Mischief Time

Four a.m.
A faint cry.
Doves.

I lie still.

Sometimes a phrase
A single word
A line

Insistent.

Unless I keep still
They tumble out
Running this way and that.

Sometimes all there
Lines in place
Images
Shape.

I do not know
If badgering works
But keep faith
With that first cry.

The Unconstrained

'It is not a landscape without figures.'

The hounds of mockery kept yapping at his heels:
Fourteenth child. Willie Come Lately. No matter
How he turned he could not miss the smirk.
Got in the master's barn, dropped by the hen
astray between the pews of parson and priest.
Indulged in one, falsely placed in the other
with no where to lay his head, a month here
a month there, with no one to answer to.
Well beaten but never taught, he picked up enough
to wipe the credulous eye and not be fooled.
Without a hearth to call his own he made
the valley his home. Never absent from dance
or wake, head and tail of every sport
had an eye for the girls, took the Ribbon oath
knew curses and cures, gossip and slander, his head
in the clouds, his feet stuck in the turf.

Everywhere he went he felt derision.
White-blackbird. Beast with five legs.
Never sure which way to turn, his mother's
pet, his sister's get, his father's brat.
A spoiled pup, answerable to no one. Half-wit
fool, braggart, a match for any man.
He shirked the Munster test, thought he could walk
on water, was duped along the pilgrim path
suffered the sting of clerical disregard.
A soft child who could not take the knock
and struck back with the only weapon he had.

The years went by, the girls went by, they knew
which side his bread was buttered on, without
a spade to call his own, educated and useless.
His only gift the gift of the gab. Coxcomb.
His father's son, finding a track in the roots
of his mind, in the half-lost, in a broken world.
All he need do was bring it up, record.
A trade to be learnt, a voice to be found, two worlds
to be joined. He served his time to elegance
the balanced phrase, the poise, ways of speech
that limmed the speaker's world. Taste, education.
The more he learnt, the more he felt discrepancy.

Dropped in the valley, he never tried to deny
what happened then. Reared to lawlessness.
Aware of injustice, Orangemen battering the door
bayonets prodding the bed. Maimed from the start.
What could he do but follow a flawed style
fit himself out in the rags of pretence, ape
the master, adapt to jaw busting, tongue
twisting, become the boy on the hired horse?
Like a cuckoo chick he ate more than his share
took advantage of love, drew sibling ire.
His self-portrait bites the hand that writes.
He carried it off, brought his crooked soul
to a crooked place, kissed the girl good-bye
denied feeling and when the harm was done
slunk back, married the girl he left behind.
Iced a fruitless cake with sentiment.

Rotten water outside every door.
Steaming dunghill, cesspool, the slip of a pig.
He put it down in shameful, hurtful candour.
It could not be in vistas, planned perspectives
porticos, broken columns, arcades.

But central, his, his people, as much part of him
as his halved mind and broken sensibility.
It was not a landscape without figures.
Loony master, spoiled priest, the big word
in the big mouth, ragged female, forelocks
touched, caps raised, urchins smirking.
The man on the horse riding above the stench.

The story scalded inside like hot stirabout.
Soured. He saw it raw, he saw it whole.
He felt the challenge. Horror. Guilt. Not
to get mired, to keep the midden at arm's length.
Not to stand on the hill, his nose stuck in the air.
The mind turned in upon itself. Desecration
the priest of chaos fingering the host
swearing a black oath on the white book.
He got it right, felt it right, the shift
to common speech, that hinge that let both sides in
grotesque, before the descent. Reprisal. Murder.
The woman's head in flames, father and child
pitched back, conflagration making the sky sublime.
He will show them through the arched eye,
the mannered voice, so unnaturally attuned
to action outside the norm, to darkness at the heart.
These are the unconstrained. Hell's angels
loose in the night, mirrored by water, intent.

'To the divil I pitch slavery.' He could not put it
mildly. He saw the abyss that gaped between
what had been and now was, between
what his father had and he had not, a belonging
the past laid out in strips, a pedlar's pack
of song, story, custom, what the memory held.
The valley drained, stilled. It was up to him
not to forget, to look into the chasm, to hear the voice
of the man beside the clevvy, the actor-narrator.

Found it intractable, made mistakes, lurched
into melodrama, made things improbably right.
It was as though what he felt exceeded
what he could do, his sense of things so clear
they could not be brought down to slate accountancy.
Two voices matched divisions in his mind
spoke of barn and hovel, matched the rift
as though within his work, in contradiction
and counterpoint, he plumbed both sides of himself.

White blackbird. Beast with five legs.
Even at the end he could not put it right.
Against the odds he made a shape that holds.
The world he drew, the field others tilled
reworked through time, now gone beyond constraint.

Post-haste

Until the books arrived I had not known how much
I had wanted to see them, to take pleasure
in sight and touch and smell, to wallow in joy
to put an end to cursed tightlippedness.

I've done my time, made a third, avoided
friendships, weighted my tongue against sneaks.
Five years of that put a stop to spontaneity.
Excitements of the mind stuck in the mind.

Today I'm stirred by the postman's knock
moved to act, to send copies to Oregon
Norfolk, Ballycastle, to act while feeling lasts
not to give love a second thought.

My love, my love

I love it when he is as courteous
at dawn as at any other hour

drags himself out of bed
with a look of dismay

when I say 'hurry, it's almost day
no one must find you here'

he sighs as though his heart would break
the night, he implies, was much too brief

once up he does not hurry into his clothes
but whispers and lingers behind my ear

raising the blind we look out
how can he face the day on his own?

When to the sessions

In carts and traps they came to his door
With a shout and a slap beasts changed hands.
They talked of crops, animals, prices
He put his ear to every gap.
They talked of politics and politicians
He had a word to the wise.
The dying child asked for him
The woman dead by her own hand carried into the house.
He dressed a wound that never healed.

Little tasks brought us close – gathering sticks
Going for milk, cycling to Sunday Mass.
The bigger tasks were even better.
I pushed the barrow from the dung heap
Helped to fork it steaming and fresh into the bottoms.
I proved my worth that day
Yet now doubt the achievement.
Was I strong enough to wheel the barrow along the path
Up the yard, onto the risen ground? Of this I am more certain:
We faced each other across a fallen tree
Entered the give and take, dust pouring out
As we cut. Above our heads trees blew back
And forth, the breeze came in from Longleg and Rockabill.
Crows circled, birds darted, the dog took it all in.
It was good, it was strong. Even better when we began
To split the logs. He swung the big axe high, forced massive
wedges into the wood when knots refused to crack.
I loved the sound of splintering, the clean rasping
The cracking, the tearing apart, loved placing smaller wedges
Where I could swing the lesser sledge. Man's work.
What I did I did well, a smaller version of what he did.
I showed my mettle. I believe that working together
Is as much an expression of closeness as anything

That might be said. When we raked the gravel on each side
	of the avenue
Twin ovals curving to the iron gates, he would rake
And I would rake, drawing the teeth inward
Making a pattern, the rhythm of our movements
Parallel and equal, the sweep not equal but each contributing.
It was companionable. He could not handle the language
	of praise
Affection, encouragement, love's avowal.

A child died, grief gagged the grave. Who can measure
The tenacity, the clamping? Such death chilling the blood
Can make a man determined never again to be torn.
We had those years. Afterwards the widening.
Education takes the child from the nest
Puts obstacles between the familiar and the acquired.
It becomes difficult to have a rhythm back
and forth, to draw parallel lines in casual motion.
I saw it happening but could do nothing to prevent.
At lunch one day we had nothing to say.

After a day's work he gardened by lamplight
Making drills, planting, transplanting shoots of lettuce
From a wooden box, enticing tomatoes behind a piece of glass
Giving rhubarb a head start beneath a half barrel –
He knew what went on in the dark. I have to think of this side
That made him strip and set to in poor light
Children in bed, unaware of night labour.
Only the lady with the lamp understood.
I can fit the story of his life on one page
Yet it runs in my mind, remembered, reconstructed, imagined
The gap incalculable, perspectives skewed
Obscured by feeling, distorted by interpretation.

In the scales of recollection I must place brazen rings –
Beggar My Neighbour, Snap, Ludo, Snakes and Ladders, Marbles.
Even then I knew he joined in because I needed companionship.
Because I fussed he took me with him on a bitter night
　　to Bearnagaoire.
I knew it was wrong and paid the sick price.
He could sing and she could sing and I could sing
Yet we never had a singsong, an evening session
A dawn chorus, a midday round, never gave way.

Had I taught in the local school
He could have measured that by old sanction.
I could have managed, walked the dog along the Skerries Road
Drank pints with the lads in The White Hart.
But even that would not have knitted us.
There is no turning back, no restitching, nothing as tangible
as skill and craft, the warmth of worn hands.
I do what I can to get a picture that makes sense
Or half-sense. My ineptitude easy to explain, his
Judgement on it harsh and accurate. In his terms
I was useless. About us were men and women
Who had what it takes. When our wall collapsed a neighbour
Got sand and cement, mixed them, got the right number of blocks
Bedded them down course by course and closed the gap.

Men knew how to wield the scythe, fork hay, fix gutters
release drains, paint, replace slates.
When something needed to be done there was always someone
　　to do it.
The sexton rang the funeral bell, gravediggers stepped to the task.
What I absorbed had little to do with these.
I never gave him the satisfaction of doing what he could admire.

In a process I could not control I was taken away.
Something was there from the start.
Those I admired shared thoughts, had words for feelings.
He made no comment, neither yea nor nay.
I went away, came back, went off again, came back.
By then he was dead, taking his silence with him.
I cannot tell how it was between us at the end.
I had my ticket, would see him one more time, but he did
    not wait.
The Dean entered my classroom, waited for me to finish.
As soon as I saw him I knew what he had to say.
I had gone too far. I had let him down.
We would never get to the bottom of this.

The Gentle Years

They never told me what was wrong with you
Just took you off in the dark to that ugly ward
Where you lapsed at once into a silent place
Neither doctors nor nurses could infiltrate
Where you closed the shutters of your mind
On guard against intrusion, let them do what they might
Let them peer and probe, tap chest and back
You kept your counsel, held your peace, even
When I sat for hours beside the bed, silent too
We had no need for words, not now, not ever
Respecting your decision to opt out, to dwindle
Softly out of sight, no need for fuss, that
Was not your style, nor mine, like-minded
Until one day I found you wide awake
And smiling, happy to see me, ready to talk
I said, 'wait here, don't go way, I'll get
Maura', and hurried off to bring my wife
Your gift to her as to me, time for parting
Time for love, for thoughtfulness, before the end
Before you went back into that silent place
And I resumed my quiet watching by your side
Until once again in the dead of night
They summoned me and Authority at the door
Questioned my rite of passage and I felt the rage
Bursting, it drove straight out of my mouth
I told him savagely I was going upstairs
To see my mother die, that shut him up
And there you were breathing softly still, dwindling
Down, in need of nothing, little Red Riding Hood
Come quick, the woods, the shore, breathing while
I watched and waited, we needed no one, in
our secret place, dug-out of memories, until
reminding me you scrunched your face, not liking

the taste, and quietly went. I waited a moment
then went to tell them they could run in now
with book and candle, clatter about the bed
do things you did not need, your soul was safe
and had been so through all our gentle years.

When Love Is Not Enough

She keeps to herself
Has her meals brought to her room
Berates the staff
Visitors are not welcome.

She complains to her children –
'they never come to see her
their visits are too short
why didn't they come earlier
when she could have enjoyed their visit?

She has nothing to wear
her shoes need repair
the heels are worn
the toes bare
do they think she can live
in the same old rags day after day?' –

Once when I found her turned to the wall
she asked why I came to see her
all I could think of saying was, 'Because I love you'.

After a brief silence I heard her say
with unanswerable conviction
'love is not enough.'

The Winding Stair

Upriver someone from my part of the country
is being tried for beating his wife to death.

Over lunch our friend reveals he has found a letter
inside a book he bought from a woman in Italy

To a man in Dublin asking why she has not heard from him.
She encloses a photograph. She is darkly attractive.

A woman recalls how her late husband
drew women about him with his conversation.

But since he never talked with her
she often wonders why he had chosen her.

Her friend has the answer: 'You were beautiful.
He loved you for your beauty. There is also companionship.'

She and her husband have just read *The Dark Labyrinth*
discussing it in detail. Her eyes are shining as she speaks.

The conversation goes beyond us, as always
when it touches on love's ferocious intricacy.

Slipstream

Stuntman of the skies, formation flying
over the sea from Gormanstown, banking
into the sun, the mountains of Mourne turning
to roam the air with you, the great plain

leveling beyond Tara and the Boyne
to where, a sweet grape-blue, Dublin's hills
are delicately scrolled towards Rockabill.
What you really loved were solo flights.

You looped the loop so many times
the watching heads were swiveled into knots.
You calmly dived beneath the Delvin viaduct
and dropped your washing home at Lusk.

Each time I see daredevils now
tricked out in goggles, leather helmets, mitts
I see you soaring, banking, dipping
shutting the engine off, dropping into

free-fall, loving the sibilant rush
of air, the land flying beneath your feet
a heart-stopping world in waiting;
then giving the engine a kiss of life

tilting upward to cones of cloud, wind-whorled
your thumb upstretched to mine, standing
scared upon Ardgillan strand
my hands miming airy turbulence.

During the War

The wood became a place of fear when once
at dusk I entered and felt a touch of dread.
A blackbird gave a warning, sharp and definite.
Someone was at the other side, a stranger
who did not want to be seen, who sensed or saw me
through the trees. He was my side
of the low wall that bounded the demesne.
A bird spoke, the trees leaned close, I stopped.
Later I heard a parachute was found
signs of a camp, an empty tin, a shoe.

I made a hideaway by throwing bits
of timber across a ditch and covering them
with sacks and rags. I liked to crouch inside.
Once when it started to rain I sheltered there.
Drips fell from the trees in a soft plopping.
Trickles of moisture began to come down the bank
to form eddies that gathered and gained force
to carry away leaves and bits of twig.
Rain drove at the roof, trees clashed
a train hammered past, the ground shuddering.

As I hover above the trough a flotilla
looms through the fog: a convoy heading
for the supply route, putting a brave face
on bad conditions as they heave and roll.
A U-boat skulks in the depths, torpedoes loaded.
Destroyers circle, lobbing depth-charges.
Ships manoeuvre this way and that while overhead
Spitfires are tearing the sky apart, the sea
is churning, ships in a panic, decks awash
sterns upending like monsters diving to the deep.

Overhead a dogfight starts, planes diving
and screeching, pilots skillful in evasion and attack
gloved fingers poised. A plane soars
upward black smoke marking its path.
It abruptly flips and falls, the engine sputtering.
The mouth of hell has split to release a band
of demons flying planes, grinning when one
falters and plummets, and when they see a parachute
at Rockabill, they swoop guns blazing
finish him off, then roar upwards and away.

The Mischievous Boy

Most of the time the boy is good
He plays in the fields, plays in the woods
He has a dog who likes to run
Who leaps in the grass, who runs in the woods
Together they try to frighten the fox
Together they try to scare the hawk

Most of the time the boy is good
But some of the time he gets into trouble
He flung his shoes into the churn
He ruined the butter and dirtied the milk
He pulled the plug from the water vat
It gushed out and knocked him flat
His father carried him into the kitchen
Stripped him naked in front of the woman
And rubbed him hard from head to toe
He rubbed his back, he rubbed his bum
The visiting woman had a good look
He knows she is trying to see his mickey
When he was dressed he was asked to perform
He stuck out his chest and let her have it

One, two, three
My mother caught a flea
She put it in the teapot
To make a cup of tea
The flea jumped out
My mother let a shout
And in walked a bobby
With his shirt sticking out

Up in the Castle the Captain is ready
He stands on the steps and looks all about
He is proud of his lands, proud of his trees
This is the day he will go to town
He checks his watch, he takes his stick
Slowly walks down to the line
The man at the crossing is getting ready
Checking the flags, one red, one green

This day the boy has a lot on his mind
He has hung the finch's cage outside
And hears it singing with all of its might
He was told not to do it, told not to do it
But now he has done it and nobody knows
And the goldfinch loves its day in the sun.

The rooster struts about in the yard
He too likes to be in the sun
He has taken a fancy to one of the hens
A soft plump bird, a soft sweet chick.
He strides about, stretching his legs
And gives a resounding crow of assertion

The boy has too many things on his mind
He knows the chick wants to escape
He knows the fox is waiting to strike
He knows the hawk is making a turn
The farmyard echoes the rooster's call
Even the jackdaws pay attention
But something is wrong, the hen missing
The soft white chick has gone on the run
The boy has searched, raced here and there
Into the henhouse, down to the piggery
He has checked the garden, checked the pit
The hen has given them all the slip

The hen in fact has a mind of her own
She wants to pick between the stones
Freshly raked in front of the house
Because the Captain is going to town
She wants to wander across the fields
Where she knows there are lots of things to eat
The fox in the Dell is pricking his ears
If she comes to the fields, he's there with a chance
The hawk once again is making his rounds
He has been to the shore, has searched the cliff
Now crosses the wood, is eyeing the fields
He sees the hen but what can he do
He knows she would make a hullabaloo
She stretches her neck when she feels his shadow
If he wants to attack she will make a racket.

The Captain knows he has plenty of time
The train is leaving the nearest station

There goes the train to Dublin town
Puffing along the line
See how the wheels are turning around
See how the red light shines

The rooster gives another call
The hen has crossed into the fields
At the edge of the wood the fox is waiting
At the back of the house the hawk sweeps low
He wraps his wings about the bars
With a cling and a clatter he scrapes the wires
The finch is shrieking, dashing about
The claws are forcing the bars apart
The beak is striking hard and fast
The mischievous boy is not to be seen
The fox seizes the plump white hen

And throws her lightly across his shoulder
The mischievous boy gives a warning shout
His father reacts and follows the fox
The Captain comes to the level crossing
The mischievous boy must do his duty
He seizes the flags, red and green
Stands bravely across the·tracks
And brings the train to a shuddering halt
He helps the Captain into a carriage
Shuts the door with a mighty clap
Seizes the flag, green to go
And sends the Captain off to the city

There goes the train to Dublin town
Puffing along the line
See how the wheels are turning around
See how the red light shines

The mischievous boy has nothing to hide
Nevertheless he's in big, big trouble
The hawk is pulling the cage apart
The terrified bird is limp with fear
When the boy races out to the yard
The hawk is bright in the morning sun
The wings on fire, the eyes like lamps
The boy shouts, the hawk flees
The finch has collapsed, he might be dead
The boy knows he should not have taken him out.
Nobody wins. Even the fox loses his grip
And the hen legs it back to the yard
His father arrives all red in the face
He's not used to all this running about
Furthermore, he's all in a flutter
The cage is wrecked, the hen traumatic
The rooster has to forego his pleasure
The finch has had a heart attack

The boy's to blame for all the bother
Worst of all he hasn't a notion
Which train he waved to a shuddering halt
He stopped the first that came along
It could be going off to the zoo
It could be going to Timbuktu

All they can do is wait and see
Hope the Captain will know what to do

There goes the train to Dublin town
Puffing along the line
See how the wheels are turning around
See how the red light shines

The mischievous boy is sent to his room
They think if they keep him out of the way
The day will proceed with no more trouble
He's supposed to reflect on what he has done
Instead he is waiting for night to come
When once again he will straddle the track
Waving the lantern to and fro

He wants to know what the Captain saw
Did he go to the zoo? Did he take a tram?
Did he feed the monkeys with monkey nuts?
Or take a ride on the elephant?
Did the tigers roar? Did the peacocks cry?
Next time he might take a good little boy

There goes the train to Dublin town
Puffing along the line
See how the wheels are turning around
See how the red light shines.

In the Train

As she softly bemoaned the mist
that seemed to swathe itself about her
she might have stepped from *Ireland of the Welcomes*
in her tweed suit and Tara brooch.

She deplored the drabness of the carriage
scoffed at alien pictures, Llandudno, Windermere.
Delivered a tale of woe with an old refrain:
men out of work, the young departing.

As the countryside churned past I could see
choked ditches, roofs down, empty barns.
'There is no money,' she whispered, 'no incentive.
Only for what is sent back, people would starve.'

A Vision of Ireland in the Twenty-first Century

Accountants, bureaucrats, venture capitalists
Relentlessly moving, engineers, neurologists
Oncologists, cardiologists, plastic surgeons, crack dealers
Like crazed cattle, angry bees, disturbed ants
Taking a bus, boarding a train, calling a cab
Pharmacists, publicans, publicists, priests, hitting the road
They drive, they queue, SUVs, Porsches
Cadillacs, Opels, Toyotas, with power steering
Power brakes, air bags fit to burst
Moon roof, alloy wheels, remote control
Financial Controllers, Systems Analysts, Corporate
Finance Executives, Senior Reconciliations Administrators
Mounting the stairs, using the lifts, manning the desks
To use the iPhones, the iPods, the TV streamers
Makers, shakers checking the Nasdaq and the Hang Sen
Hunter-gatherers, stab merchants, up for a killing

Song of Our Time

Cayman, Cayman
Cayman rock
Hand me your money
You'll never get caught.

Jersey, Jersey
Jersey shore
Give me the lolly
I know the score.

I'm a one-man bank
A classy act
Your money goes in
Your money comes back.

To me you're a number
One, two, three
Nothing in writing
Not even the fee.

In for a penny
In for a pound
Now can you hear
That Seychelles sound?

Don't tell your mammy
Don't tell your son
Keep it tight
Have some fun.

Buy another house
Buy another yacht
Be seen at the races
Be seen at the spot.

Go with the best
Go with the flow
It's a golden circle
Of those in the know.

Cayman, Cayman
Cayman rock
Seychelles, Seychelles
Seychelles!

Lost for Words

The affliction is common now.
When asked to verify a particular event
Bankers, businessmen and politicians
Confess to being unable to do so.
When asked to identify a signature
Stare at the hand as at a foreign member.

They can, they say, only presume
That if the cheque bears their signature
They must have signed it, but they have
No recollection of signing
No knowledge of where the money went
– Seychelles, Cayman Islands, Jersey?

ii

At Question Time the Taoiseach
Hides behind a beaten bush:
'In so far as I could
with little available records
I am satisfied
Having spoken to the person
Who administered the account
That it was used
For bona fide purposes
That the cheques
Were prepared by that person
And countersigned by another party member.
Their purpose was to finance personnel
Press and other normal supports
For an opposition leader.
There was no surplus and no misappropriation…'.

iii

At a meeting in London
Our man cuts to the chase:
'I hope that in a spirit
Of co-operation and friendship
We can surmount
Any problems that may arise
To ensure that the peace and stability
We have striven to achieve
Endures for future generations
And is paralleled by a process
Of healing and of reconciliation.'

iv

Explaining the delay in hearing evidence
The Chairman of the Tribunal spoke
Of a disposition on the part of a number of financial institutions
Involving protracted and convoluted correspondence
And tardiness or non-compliance in relation to orders
Which he had to say appeared unhelpful
And lacking in due co-operation.

v

The Taoiseach explains why a Minister was not told.
'In relation to Minister O…'s department
or my own department, I mean,
there are sometimes,
for some reason or other,
something isn't brought to the attention of all the relevant people,
whether that's the Taoiseach, or Minister, or Minister of State
or some public servant – there will be reports done in that case –
but I have to say, in fairness, in every department it is complex,
there's a huge range of issues going on
and I would always defend those involved in them
because it is so easy,

I mean, when I walk the corridor to here,
I'm everyday, I'm everyday and back, caught by officials
and well, – is it all right to me we move on this?
or what we'd said last week at a cabinet committee
or there's this meeting in Northern Ireland,
or there's this meeting in Europe –
and I give instant decisions –
if I was to think every time,
then some official goes in,
puts that all in an e-mail,
if you were to show me that in two months,
you know, the complexities that are involved in that,
the only thing I find – you would,
wouldn't take this away from me –
is watching this: how everyone is having so much difficulty
remembering what happened a month ago
and the eminent people in another location
expecting me to answer
remember everything with certainty
what happened 17 years ago,
but that's maybe they credit me more intelligence than
everyone else,
but anyway…
I, I, I, well; I don't think it's that,
I don't mention, remember everything …
eh, but it is difficult, but that's part of the,
that's part of the system,

I think if you're making decisions like that
some things go wrong.
I honestly think we have a Civil Service
that do our very, very best
to avoid any of these issues,
admittedly some things go wrong,
but it's not, it's not, I think anything
that is ever other than people
doing their very best in their job.'

vi

The Minister of State for the Environment
Tried to keep his head above water
All the initial reports were good.
No toxins. No carcinogens.

Then scientists talked about levels of
Methyl ethyl this and chloro-benzene that.
What goes up, they said, must come down.
Where on earth could he wash his hands?

vii

This is serious. The Minister for the Environment
Would impose more stringent laws to govern
Drink and driving. Harsher penalties. The right
To pursue suspects into house and home.

Deputies would not accept this break with the Past.
Think of the unfortunate farmer-drinker, they said
at the end of the day miles and miles from the pub
with only tractor or car to drive him to drink.

What can he do when midnight shuts him down?
Endanger his life walking dark roads?
Risk being run-over by drunken neighbours?
What taxi can he flag so far from town?

Even worse. Will the unfortunate man
Who bolts for home, with his car in bits
Have his door kicked in on foot of a couple of beers?
Ghastly words. Deputies roared at the bar.

A Politician's Defence

A certain type of man will want to draw about him
Certain like-minded people
Capable of appreciating the things he appreciates
Able to understand the purpose of what he does
And the significance

There is a satisfaction to be gained from having people about him
Who accept what he does and share a certain regard for him
Have that in common
They are an elite and benefit from that closeness
You see it in history
In Elizabethan houses, in the Anglo-Irish
An aesthetic achieved in architectural design
In shaping estates
Formal gardens, walks, vistas
Communion between the individual and nature
A philosophy, a moral and natural character
That found expression in their houses

It has been my intention and my privilege
To have been imbued with a sense of style
To have appreciated good art, great books
To have striven over the years to make my house an extension
    of myself
To make my way of life indicative not only of personal values
But of who and what I am
No division between my life and my work
My standing aesthetically realised
I never have known this to be understood

Did they ask the Medici if they were beholden?
Did they ask the Right Honorable John Beresford, known as
    'King of Ireland'

If he was beholden?
His life was a masterpiece
He made this house a thing of beauty
Employed Gandon
Planned the alteration to the city
I do not hear anyone putting question marks over that

There are certain men, certain types of men
Whom others are prepared to facilitate
Sometimes a particular politician
Perhaps a visionary
Someone who has a definite view
May experience financial difficulties

A situation may develop where a group of friends
Would come together to assist him
These are public-spirited people who subscribe
Disinterested people, altruistic people
They do not anticipate favours in return

Because the individual is running the country well
Keeping its finances in order
Ensuring a fair distribution of services
Seeing into the future
Engaged in initiatives that are beneficial to all
These business friends, disinterested supporters
Who drive the country forward
Creating wealth and opportunity for all
May help the individual to get him out of a spot of bother

It is easier than many realise for a politician
To get into financial difficulties
He has election expenses, campaign expenses
Not having time to look after number one

So preoccupied with matters of Government
With affairs of State
And increasingly these days with international responsibilities
He may neglect his own interests

In these perfectly understandable circumstances
He may accept assistance from others financially more fortunate
There is no ulterior motive
No compromise of the high standards such a man sets himself

Song of the Nettle Man

My last summer in the old place I saw a tinker man
Flinging handfuls of nettles into the air
Declaring to all who passed 'if you gently pluck a nettle …'.

In the pub Little Jack's stringy neck stretched
And slackened as he emptied glass after glass
While the Long Hand stayed on and on as though reluctant
To go back where half his roof had fallen in.
Through a haze of smoke the Weasel Farrell sang the song he
    always sang
'You'll never miss a mother's love till she's buried beneath the clay'
And Red Ned Connor recorded what he knew to be true
'The only man ever thrun me was Casey from Cahirciveen.'

After a day forking hay on the moat the Wolf Russell
Hurried out to the Green as music and dancing began.
They were doing fox trots and old time waltzes
But Matt the Grocer backed the sexton's maid to the pound wall
Where she gave in to his rummaging remarking
As she pulled her knickers back 'I don't know what yez do see in it.'

Couples sought privacy in the lane beyond the tinkers' camp.
Some weary of cracked cement and one accordion
Went to the Gala Dance in town where Mick Delahunty
Quickened the Square with trumpet and sax.

The nettle man sang song after song to himself
Then whispered as I went my way
'Cé hé sin amu go bhuil faobhar ar a guth?'

IV

No Contest

I can outsneeze anyone I know.
Sitting, standing, walking, inside or out.
In the car, the bus, the train, anywhere.

Earache, blocked nose, stricken eyes.
No one knows what to do with me.
Doctors, healers, quacks, I've seen them all.

Dust, bed mites, fluff, dog hair, cat fur,
spores, pollen, hot air, drafts, chills.
Any of these can set me off. Away.

Eight, nine, ten, eleven. I'm off.
Who knows when I'll ... Twelve, thirt. That'll do.
Atchoo! Atchoo! Atchoo! Atchoo! ...

Time Share

Fair game as we raise snouts in old squares
ramble along narrow streets, or pause to drown
our eyes in the blue sea, love lost in time
in man's irresistible venturing. It is then
they approach, beguile with offers of free travel
holidays in distant places, a chance to see exotic life.

In this garden by the antique sea the apple's pendulum
sways before our faces, we are caught off guard.
Is it only because we are sun-struck and out of our lives
that we are taken in by blandishments, listen
to siren voices, indulge the childlike girl
who fills the form for us, our passport to variation?

Deep down we know it is not to be
even a thatched abode by the China Sea
but we are moidered by sun and sea, half-think
that just this once there might be something for nothing
that just for once the old expulsion might not work
that this time it is our turn.

A Matter of Time

It is only a matter of time before leaves
loosen, roots drag from the earth
only a matter of time before we start
to query the fragility of air, the pace of blood
thrumming across the bone, once the evidence
shows, empty pews, missing voices
a friend hurried off in the night
only a matter of time before earth
closes about us and leaves turn to mould

The Trees at Ferrycarrig

In doomed relief they have stood in the mud
drained and bare but when the tide draws in
their slender arms are chaste and spare.

They are the trees poets made emblems of
either could stand with Lear on the doomed earth
either could play a part for Estragon.

In the moon's light their limbs appear in thin outline.
Birds have left these spectral resting places
frigid haunts, gaunt memorials.

An ice-cold wind creeps on the ravenous air
the sea has an eerie attitude, a bleak finality.
The trees inscribe a stark apocalypse.

At Water's Edge

As they talked he reached down and slowly
extracted a piece of grass from a dense tuft
the soil yielding to pressure, reluctantly
and laid it on the pool where it drifted to one side.

As they continued he stretched down again
and gently withdrew another stem from soil
that seemed to respond more readily as though
beginning to go along with these translations.

This second extraction fitted onto the other
so that by degrees the grassy source gave up
its hoard and the sea's gathering began
to assume a different order risen on water.

She perceived each stalk as it was drawn
flesh-pale below the green, flecks of clay
trailing roots bereft of cover and imagined
the silent pang of each fresh separation.

Yet felt no diminishment, neither weakened
nor ravished in this repositioning of things previously
knotted as though nothing were coming into being
beyond slight adjustments, neither here nor there.

A World Regained

i.m. John V. Kelleher (1916-2004)

Since your people played the emigrant's game
you took the pilgrim track to Clondrohid and Derrnagree.
When you crested Watergrasshill you felt confirmed.

Pines, stone houses, the Nagles, Blackwater.
In Cork searched out lanes and streets to get
the feel of places known through novel and tale.

In Dublin met the gluggers who shook their fists
at church and state. When they pulled the bellman's
rope you knew what dragged beneath their feet.

In Grafton Street you felt the poet's scorn.
Beside the bridge you met the mournful man
and understood the grit beneath the nails.

For forty years you showed the way, unabashed
by word stoppage, standing squarely at the desk
right hand thrusting downward repeatedly.

You cracked the *Wake*, recited Yeats, sang songs
drew story after story from your mind's hoard
counterpointing fiction with the hard core of fact.

You had your secret life, the backward look
time's waste grist to your mind. In the end
charts and notebooks held a world regained.

Day Care Centre

Brought by ambulance, taxi, or minibus
they enter the long room, one by one
some in wheelchairs, some on walking frames
their spirits taking the lift.
They have made it again, meet again.
They joke, spin yarns, talk of family, go back over things.
Enjoying the fun nurses go among them, ticking names
taking blood pressure, checking the pulse
arranging a doctor's visit.
Some go to the gym where they inch along
fearful and anxious gripping bars
others turn wheels, limbering up, do the bicycle jaunt
or lie back to have their legs massaged.
Here nobody raises the bar, nobody pumps iron.
It might seem they are too old or too far gone
that they ought to be back home, feet to the fire.
But no, they have left their rooms and bed-sits
fared forth at the State's expense.
Here they are equals, with dodgy tickers, lung disease
high blood pressure, shakes, spasms, dizzy spells.
No matter, this is the republic of the day care centre.
Week after week they sing the same songs
Have you ever been lonely?
Have you ever been blue?
They let it out, clap hands, release the rebel yell.
This is their day of days, their weekly come and get it.

They also serve

The mixer leans its long neck down and slobbers
out a gush of pale cement two men
push back and forth within a wooden frame.
The job is quickly done. Machines move off.

One man remains, guardian of the slow completion.
He stands at ease, looking up the road
or down, and seems to have no thought of what
comes next. In the depths of his mind nothing stirs.

It is not idleness although it may seem so
to those who come and go, driving at speed
or those who slowly walk children to school
or those who hurry past with shopping bags.

He has emptied his mind and holds his ground
when it might be thought he should be somewhere else
with something to do but his task is to be here
doing nothing at all, and doing it well.

Fish

Because last year was cold and melancholy
I neglected them, left their food undisturbed
Let the pond go weedy and sullen.

This year I feared they were dead
Yet filled the watering can and poured it out
In a long spiralling cascade.

Red shapes began to blur beneath its spill.
I scattered flakes of fresh food.
They began to feed, brilliant heads rising one by one.

I counted three, then four and a mysterious white.
Next day I gave more water and more food.
Counted eight, then nine, ascending

To the splash, gulping, avid for life.
They have slept in mud, survived winter's discontent
Earned their right to our worldly satisfactions.

I love their strength, their capacity to grow
Despite the odds, to overcome restrictions
And disregard slow decline.

Counting Chairs

There's someone who doesn't want to talk about me.
I woke up one morning and decided to count
The number of chairs in the house
That could seat two people.
There were six.
Then I got up and went about the house
Counting them
And there were eleven.
Five more than I had thought.
Next day I told someone about this
And she went about her house
And counted the chairs
In which two people could sit
Comfortably.
She has, she told me, rather a lot
And went into detail
About Chesterfields, wing backs, cane chairs
And the set her father bought from Lady
Autumnbottom
When she sold Hampton Hall
Before she left for the colonies
Beautiful pieces, priceless treasures.
Then she told a friend
And how the idea had started with me
And the friend said 'if you mean that fellow
Who lectures at UCD on the Romantic Poets
I don't want to talk about him.'
I don't know why she won't talk about me
Or about chairs.

V

I speak in stone.

i

Walk the incline to the Temple of Deir El Bahari
Start your voyage to the Land of God
Anchor quietly in the desert of Punt
Bring back my incense trees

ii

With Amoun's help
I did not neglect
the place of origin
the horizon of earth
the great hill of beginning
the god's eye

Beside the pylon
in the sacred court
I speak to the sky
I wear the white crown
I shine in the red
My rule touches the ends of the sky
Where the sun shines is mine

iii

Queen of the Two Lands
the chaste egg
reared by the Great Pair
I have done what no one has ever done

Crowned with electrum
my slender obelisks
stand on the first mound
shine beneath the stars
flood the Two Lands with light

Wadi El Natroun

Once thousands came to taste these brackish pools
now hundreds strict in sandals and black robes
affirm their faith along the Desert Road.

These Coptic sages do things by degrees
first try out solitude in cells nearby
then dwell far-off among desolate dunes.

When raiders hacked and razed they wiped
their swords beside the Martyrs' Well.
When Bishoi died Patrick kept his word.

Closure at Bethlehem

Like chambered tombs of Boyne
these high and caverned halls
whose massive walls are cool
even in summertime.

Like ocean-view hotels
in wintertime the rooms
are closed, the notice boards
bare, one has a list

of classes never held.
A door ajar reveals
a blackboard dusted still
with someone's faded thoughts

and rows of empty chairs.
Next door in shrouded shapes
computers wait. The force
of silence fills the air.

Waco Padre

Outrider in a ten-gallon hat
God's wrangler, clerical big-shot
you steer a course by a lone star
God's panhandler riddling for souls.

You amble towards me through the years
as nimble-tongued as when
cross-gartered to the knees, you flung
sly kisses at a two-faced manikin.

The pose you struck withstood all tampering
the clamps, the bits, Jack Treacy's penal brand.
We drink to this and that, old hands
survivors, jokers, pardners on a roll.

Shiki

It might seem like more of what we knew:
abnegation, mortification
the body brought to luminous skin and bone
Culdees on the edge flying to God
others living off berries and wild herbs
limbs stretched in their yearning to breaking point
reality itself imagined as an aspect of His creation.

'On my sick bed
I feel like dew
falling on the earth.'

Here there is no penitential zeal
The affliction has not been chosen
Nor has it been welcomed
From a cramped position, within a narrow angle
The little bird sings his way to the bitter end.

A seeing, a getting through
A private syllabic measuring.

'Oh, Morning Glory
My heart races
Wishing to sketch you!'

His bones rotted, his gums festered
His seven wounds discharged
In a five-mat room he crawled from one futon to another.

Sleepless, sobbing
Depressed when no one came to see him.

'I scream, I scream.
How I scream! How I weep!'

He cried out when they changed his dressings.

When a dead man called
He sketched the instruments of release.

All he had was a portion of sky
A few clumps of white chrysanthemums.
He made do with dearth.

'I can see, I can see
The pine in my garden I can see.'

He gave his mind to what he had
Valued rice porridge, salted plums, cocoa, bonito, chicken loaf
Socks on the line
The tips of the begonias
The transience of the bottle gourd.

A morning glory withered
Before he could finish painting it.

This is not what we used to imagine
Great spirits sojourning
Mighty ferment
An infusion of personal passion
Transforming the ordinary.

The gods are missing.
History is somewhere else.

It comes down to one man
His sketches and poems.

One man lying, viewing, marvelling
A concentration in sharp recoil.

'When the blood rushes to my head
I cannot open my eyes.

Since I cannot open my eyes
I cannot read newspapers.

Since I cannot read newspapers
I just keep thinking.

I know that death is coming.

Since I know that death is coming
I want to enjoy myself before then.

Since I want to enjoy myself
I feel like trying some exceptional feast.

Since I feel like trying some exceptional feast
I need something to occupy myself with.

Since I need something to occupy myself with
I come to think of selling my books ...

No, no, I do not want to sell my books.
Well, then, I am in trouble.

Since I am in trouble,
The blood rushes to my head even more.'

Not the known aesthetic and meditative art.

This demands exact attention.

To observe, to capture and to reflect
The life-span of an image.

Linked to the ordinary
With no release in humour.

No indulgence of the heroic
No ironic intervention.

He attended to the silence
Behind the chirring of the cicada.

He brought the frog to our attention
Standing on one leg.

He noted:

'A kingfisher stirs his feathers
on the bough
of a Confederate rose.'

In the toughness of the heart-bamboo
He saw himself
In the brevity of gourds
In the cuckoo's witnessing.